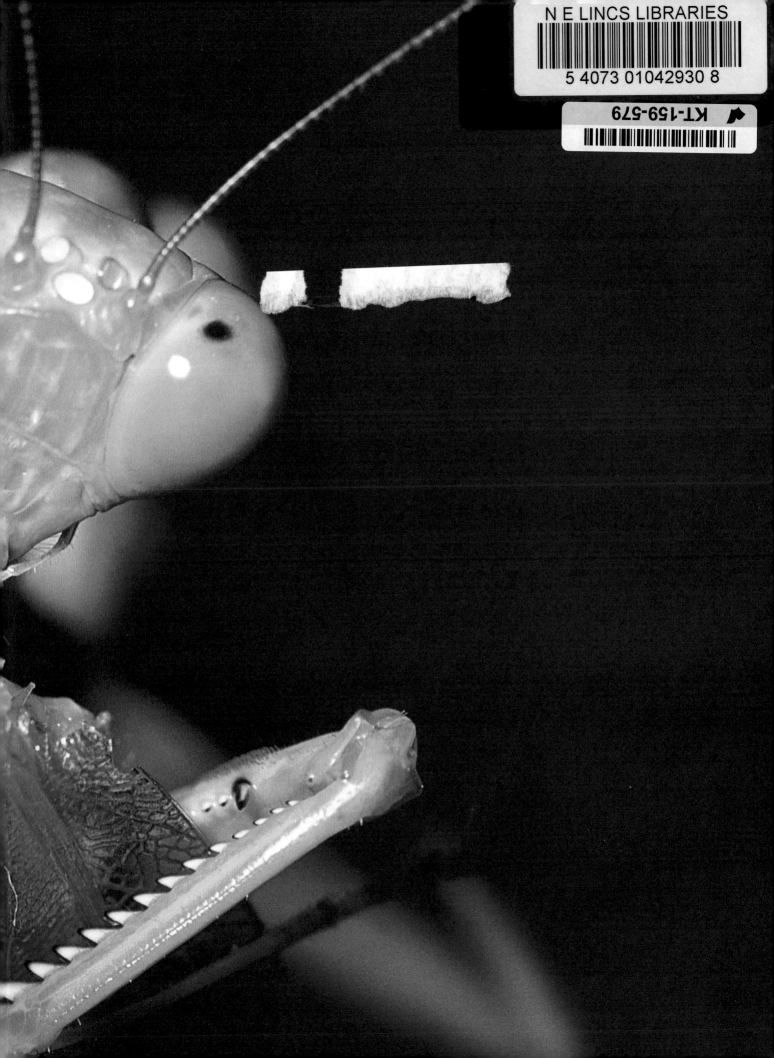

EXPLORING NATURE

BEETLES & BUGS

A captivating inside view of the life of two of the most
successful insect species on the planet, with over 200 pictures

Jen Green
Consultant: Mathew Frith

ARMADILLO

C O N

This edition is published by Armadillo, an imprint of Anness Publishing Ltd, 108 Great Russell Street, London WC1B 3NA; info@anness.com

www.annesspublishing.com

Anness Publishing has a new picture agency outlet for images for publishing, promotions or advertising. Please visit our website www.practicalpictures.com for more information.

© Anness Publishing Ltd 2014

Publisher: Joanna Lorenz
Senior Editor: Nicole Pearson
Project Editors: Dawn Titmus, Rebecca Clunes
Editor: Sarah Eason
Picture Researcher: Su Alexander
Illustrators: Stuart Carter, Rob Sheffield
Designer: Jill Mumford
Production Controller: Pirong Wang

PICTURE CREDITS
b=bottom, t=top, c=central, l=left, r=right
Heather Angel: 6tr / Art Archive: 9br, 41tl / BBC Natural History Unit: 6l, 22t, 57tl / Corbis: 1, 45tl / Ronald Grant Archive: 5tr / Kobal Collection: 55tr / NHPA: 6br, 7bl, 12c, 14t, 14bl, 15b, 16c, 19tr, 19bl, 20t, 21tl, 21br, 22b, 27t, 28c, 29b, 37b, 39tr, 42t, 43br, 50t, 51b, 52, 53tl, 53b, 58, 61br / Oxford Scientific Films: 5tl, 5br, 7t, 9t, 9bl, 11c, 11br, 15t, 15c, 17, 18r, 19br, 21tr, 21bl, 22c, 23b, 24b, 25t, 25bl, 26b, 27c, 27b, 29t, 29c, 30t, 31, 35tl, 35br, 37c, 38c, 39tl, 41tr, 41b, 43t, 44t, 45tr, 46b, 47t, 48l, 51t, 51c, 53tr, 55b, 56b, 57tr, 59t, 59br, 60, 61bl / Papilio Photographic: 19tl, 50br, 55tl, 57br / Kim Taylor: 4t, 5bl, 8br, 10, 12t, 13t, 13b, 14br, 16t, 18l, 23t, 24t, 26t, 37tr, 42b, 48r, 49t / Volkswagen: 11bl / Warren Photographic: 4b, 8bl, 11t, 12b, 13c, 16b, 20b, 23c, 25br, 26c, 28t, 28b, 30b, 32, 33, 34, 35tr, 35bl, 36, 37tl, 38t, 38b, 39c, 39b, 40, 43bl, 44b, 45b, 46t, 47c, 47b, 49b, 50bl, 56t, 57bl, 59bl, 61t.

Manufacturer: Anness Publishing Ltd, 108 Great Russell Street, London WC1B 3NA, England
For Product Tracking go to:
www.annesspublishing.com/tracking
Batch: 6787-22892-1127

T E N T S

The insects in this book are described using their **common name** first, followed by their Latin names, where known, in *italics*. When a beetle or bug does not have a common name, only its Latin name is given.

Nature's Success Story

If you were an alien visiting Earth, which creature would you consider the main life form? We humans like to think we dominate Earth, but insects are far more successful. There are over one million different species (kinds) of insects, compared to just one human species.

Scientists divide insects into groups called orders. The insects in each order share certain features. Beetles and bugs are two major insect orders. The main difference between them is that beetles have biting jaws and bugs have sucking mouthparts. Beetles are the largest order of all. So far, 350,000 different kinds of beetles and 55,000 different kinds of bugs have been found.

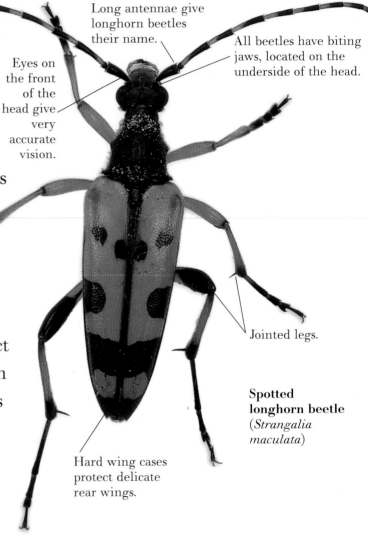

Long antennae give longhorn beetles their name.

All beetles have biting jaws, located on the underside of the head.

Eyes on the front of the head give very accurate vision.

Jointed legs.

Spotted longhorn beetle (*Strangalia maculata*)

Hard wing cases protect delicate rear wings.

▲ THE BEETLE ORDER
Beetles belong to the order Coleoptera, which means 'sheath wings'. Most beetles have two pairs of wings. The tough front wings fold over the delicate rear wings to form a hard, protective sheath. Longhorn beetles owe their name to their long antennae (feelers), which look like long horns.

◀ LIVING IN WATER
Not all beetles and bugs live on land. Some, like this diving beetle (*Dytiscus marginalis*), live in fresh water. The diving beetle hunts underwater, diving down to look for food on the stream bed.

◀ FEEDING TOGETHER

A group of aphids feeds on a plant stem, sucking up liquid sap. Most beetles and bugs live alone, but a few species, such as aphids, gather together in large numbers. Although they do not form a community, as ants and bees do, living in a group does give some protection from predators.

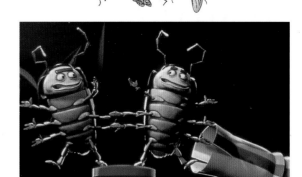

What's in a Name?

This image comes from the animated feature film A Bug's Life. *The hero of the cartoon is not actually a bug at all, but an ant. True bugs are a particular group of insects with sucking mouthparts that can slurp up liquid food.*

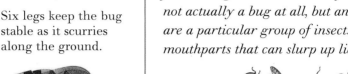

Forest shield bug
(*Pentatoma rufipes*)

Six legs keep the bug stable as it scurries along the ground.

Antennae for touching and smelling.

Thin wing-tip.

Hard wing base.

Tube-like mouthparts under the insect's head.

Eyes on the front of the head.

◀ THE BUG ORDER

Bugs come in many shapes and sizes. All have long, jointed mouthparts that form a tube through which they suck up liquid food, like a syringe. Their order name is Hemiptera, which means 'half-wings'. The name refers to the front wings of many bugs, such as shield bugs, which are hard at the base and flimsy at the tip. With their wings closed, shield bugs are shaped like a warrior's shield.

THE YOUNG ONES ▶

Young beetles, called grubs or larvae, look very different from adult beetles. A young cockchafer (*Melolontha melolontha*) feeds on plant roots in the soil. Almost all young beetles and bugs hatch from eggs. They pass through several stages in their life cycle.

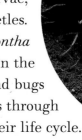

Did you know? Insects are unique in having six legs – three on either side.

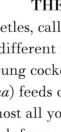

All Kinds of Beetles

One in every five animals on Earth is a beetle. These insects owe much of their success to their natural hard shells, which protects them against attack. Beetles are found all over the world, except in Antarctica and in the oceans. Long-nosed weevils, ground beetles, ladybirds, scarabs and glowing fireflies are all major beetle groups.

Goliath beetle
(Goliathus goliatus)

◄▲ LARGEST AND SMALLEST
Beetles come in various sizes. Goliath beetles from Africa (left) are the largest beetles, and one of the largest insects of all. They grow up to 15cm (6in) in length and weigh up to 100g (¼lb). At the other end of the scale, feather-winged beetles are tiny – under 1mm (¹⁄₁₆in) long and smaller than a pinhead. Hairy-winged dwarf beetles are only 0.25mm (¹⁄₆₄in) long. The tiny beetles (above) are foraging in a flower.

Hercules beetle
(Dynastes hercules)

SCARY SIGHT ►
Hercules beetles are named after the Classical Roman hero Hercules, who was famous for his strength. The tough, curved cuticle on the male's head forms huge horns, which he uses to fight and frighten away other males.

Desert scarab
(Scarabidae)

Weevil
(Curculionidae)

▲ BRIGHT AND BEAUTIFUL

This beetle is a desert scarab from western USA. There are more than 20,000 species in the scarab family alone. Most are brown, black, green or red, but some are gold, blue or plain white. Scarab beetles are an important part of the food chain because they eat dung, returning its nutrients to the soil.

▲ LONG-NOSED WEEVILS

Weevils are the largest family of beetles. There are over 40,000 species. They are also called snout beetles, because of their long noses that scientists call rostrums. The beetle's jaws, and sometimes its eyes, are found at the tip of the long snout. The antennae are often positioned halfway down the beetle's rostrum.

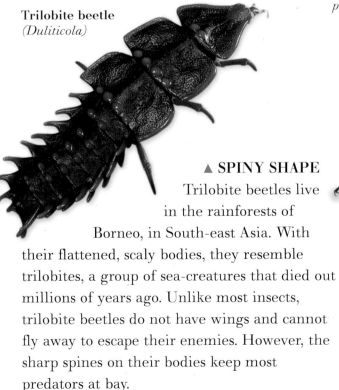

Trilobite beetle
(Duliticola)

Fiddle beetle
(Mormolycei
phyllodes)

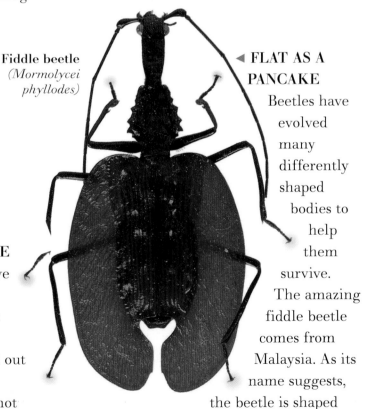

◀ FLAT AS A PANCAKE

Beetles have evolved many differently shaped bodies to help them survive. The amazing fiddle beetle comes from Malaysia. As its name suggests, the beetle is shaped like a violin. Fiddle beetles are almost flat, which helps them slip between the flat bracket fungi on the trees in which they live.

▲ SPINY SHAPE

Trilobite beetles live in the rainforests of Borneo, in South-east Asia. With their flattened, scaly bodies, they resemble trilobites, a group of sea-creatures that died out millions of years ago. Unlike most insects, trilobite beetles do not have wings and cannot fly away to escape their enemies. However, the sharp spines on their bodies keep most predators at bay.

Bugs of Every Kind

Like beetles, bugs live on every continent except Antarctica. They are found both on dry land and in fresh water. They are so small that they are rarely noticed by people and can survive on very little food. All bugs have piercing and sucking mouthparts, which are tucked beneath their heads when not in use. Many bugs suck juicy sap from plants. Some hunt other insects and suck their juices instead.

Bugs are made up of two large groups. True bugs form one group, whose scientific name is Heteroptera, meaning 'different wings'. Their front wings have hard bases and thin tips. True bugs include water stick insects, assassin bugs, shield bugs and bedbugs. Other bugs belong to the group Homoptera, which means 'same wings'. These bugs have one or two pairs of wings that are the same texture all over. They include leafhoppers, aphids, scale insects and cicadas.

Cicada
(Cicadidae family)

▲ BIGGEST AND SMALLEST
Cicadas are one of the largest bugs, growing up to 5cm (2in) long with a wingspan of up to 15cm (6in). Giant water bugs, also called 'toe-biters', grow up to 12cm (5in) long. The whitefly is one of the smallest bugs – at only 1mm (1⁄16in) long, it is almost too tiny to be seen by the naked human eye.

STRANGE INSECTS ▶
Like beetles, bugs vary a lot in shape. Scale insects owe their name to the hard scale that covers and protects the body of the females. Scale insects are unusual bugs. Most adult females have no legs, wings or antennae, and don't look like insects at all! The males have wings but no scale and look rather like tiny midges.

Scale insects
(Coccoidae)

Shield bug
(*Palomena prasina*)

▲ CROSSED WINGS
Shield bugs have broad, flattened bodies. This species has a dull appearance, but some are bright scarlet, blue or green. When resting, the shield bug crosses its front wings over its back so that its wing-tips overlap. From above, the wings form an X-shape by which you can identify true bugs – the Heteroptera group.

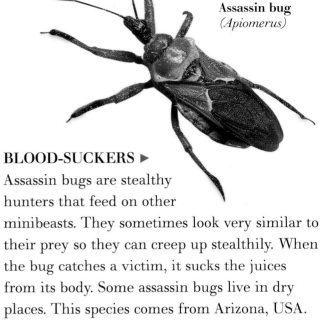

Assassin bug
(Apiomerus)

BLOOD-SUCKERS ▶
Assassin bugs are stealthy hunters that feed on other minibeasts. They sometimes look very similar to their prey so they can creep up stealthily. When the bug catches a victim, it sucks the juices from its body. Some assassin bugs live in dry places. This species comes from Arizona, USA.

▲ **WATER LOVERS**
Water stick insects (*Ranatra linearis*) live in ponds and streams. They have long, slender legs and bodies, which camouflage them from enemies. On the insect's rear is a long, thin spine, which it uses as a breathing tube. The bug draws in air from above the surface, while the rest of its body remains submerged.

▲ **LIVING LANTERN**
The lantern bug (*Fulgora*) is named for the pale tip on its snout. Although it looks like a tiny lantern, the tip does not give out light. This bug lives in the rainforests of south-east Asia. Another type of lantern bug has a huge false head, which looks like an alligator's snout.

Useful Bugs
Some types of bugs, including scale insects, are used by people. The bodies of cochineal scales can be crushed to extract cochineal, a red food dye. The Aztecs of Mexico used cochineal dye hundreds of years ago.

Body Parts

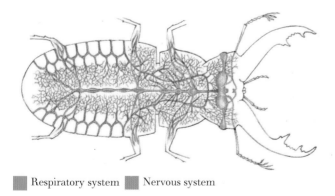

Garden chafer
(Phyllopertha horticola)

Head

Thorax

Abdomen

Human bodies are supported by a bony skeleton. Beetles, bugs and other insects have no inner skeleton. Instead, they are protected by a hard outer layer called an exoskeleton. This layer is waterproof and also helps to prevent the insect from drying out in hot weather. The exoskeleton is airtight, but it has special holes called spiracles that allow the insect to breathe.

The word 'insect' comes from a Latin word meaning 'in sections'. Like other insects, beetles' and bugs' bodies are made up of three main parts. All have a head, a thorax (middle section) and an abdomen (rear section). Almost all adult beetles and bugs have six legs, and most have two pairs of wings, which enable them to fly.

▲ THREE SECTIONS

A beetle's main sense organs, the antennae and eyes, are on its head. Its wings and legs are attached to the thorax. The abdomen contains the digestive and reproductive organs. When on the ground, the abdomen is covered by the beetle's wings.

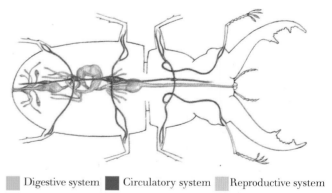

■ Respiratory system ■ Nervous system

■ Digestive system ■ Circulatory system ■ Reproductive system

▲ BREATHING AND NERVOUS SYSTEMS

The respiratory (breathing) system has spiracles (openings) that lead to a network of tubes. The tubes allow air to reach all parts of the insect's body. The nervous system receives messages from the sense organs, and sends signals to the insect's muscles to make it move.

▲ OTHER BODY SYSTEMS

The digestive system breaks down and absorbs food. The circulatory system includes a long, thin heart that pumps blood through the body. The abdomen contains the reproductive parts. Males have two testes that produce sperm. Females have two ovaries that produce eggs.

◄ IN COLD BLOOD

Like all insects, beetles and bugs are cold-blooded animals. This means that the temperature of their body is similar to their surroundings. Insects control their body temperature by moving about. To warm up, beetles and bugs bask in the sun, as this leaf beetle (Chrysomelidae) is doing. If they need to cool their bodies, they move into the shade.

SURVIVING THE COLD ►

This tiger-beetle egg (*Cicindela*) is buried in the soil. In some parts of the world, winters are too cold for most adult insects to survive. The adult insects die, but their eggs, or young, can survive in the soil because it is warmer. When spring arrives, the young insects emerge, and so the species survives.

Rhinoceros beetle
(*Megasoma elephas*)

BEETLE CAR

During the 1940s, the tough, rounded beetle shape inspired the German car manufacturer Volkswagen to produce one of the world's most popular family cars, the VW Beetle. The car's tough outer shell, just like that of a beetle, helped it to achieve a good safety record. The design proved so successful that the Beetle car was recently improved and relaunched.

▲ MOVING FORTRESS

The rhinoceros beetle is very well protected. Its tough exoskeleton covers and shields its whole body. The cuticle (outer skin) on its head forms three long points that look like a rhinoceros's horns. With all that protection, it is fairly safe for this beetle to move about!

On the Move

Beetles and bugs are expert movers. They can fly, run, leap and even swim. Some species are wingless, but most of those that have wings fly well. All adult beetles and bugs have six flexible, jointed legs, divided into four main sections. Many species have claws on their feet, which help them to cling on to smooth surfaces. Others have a flat pad between the claws, with hundreds of tiny hairs. The pads allow the insects to scramble up walls and even walk upside-down.

Squash bug
(Coreus marginatus)

▲ JOINTED LEGS

Like all beetles and bugs, squash bugs have four main sections in their legs. The top part is called the coxa, next comes the femur or upper leg, then the tibia or lower leg. The fourth section, the tarsus, is the part that touches the ground. You can also see the bug's feeding tube under its head.

▲ SPEEDY RUNNER

Tiger beetles (*Cicindela* species) are one of the fastest insects – they can cover up to 60cm (2ft) a second. As it runs, the front and hind legs on one side of its body touch the ground at the same time as the middle leg on the other side, steadying the beetle like a three-legged stool.

◀ LONG LEAPER

Leafhopper bugs (Cicadellidae family) are long-jump champions! When preparing to leap, the bug gathers its legs beneath it like a runner on the starting block. Muscles that connect the upper and lower leg contract (shorten) to straighten the leg and fling the bug into the air.

◄ SOIL SHIFTER

The burying, or sexton, beetle uses its strong front legs for digging. These ground-dwelling insects bury small animals (such as mice) in the ground to provide food for their young. The beetle's front legs are armed with little prongs that act as shovels, pushing the soil aside as it digs into the earth.

Burying beetle
(Nicrophorus humator)

ROWING THROUGH WATER ►

Great diving beetles (*Dytiscus marginalis*) are strong swimmers. Their flattened hind legs are covered with long-haired fringes, which act like broad paddles. The two back legs push together against the water, helping the insect to 'row' itself forward.

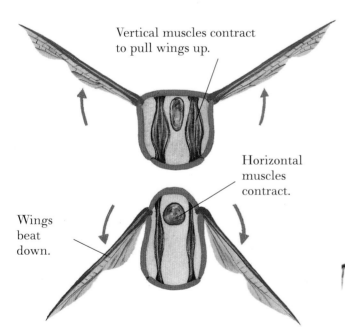

Vertical muscles contract to pull wings up.

Horizontal muscles contract.

Wings beat down.

◄ FLIGHT MUSCLES

Unlike flies, the beetle uses only its delicate rear wings for flying. Vertical muscles attached to the top and bottom of the thorax contract to flatten it. This makes the wings move up. Horizontal muscles along the body then contract to pull the thorax up, making the beetle's wings flip down. The action of the thorax controls the wings and propels the insect along.

Spotted longhorn
(Strangalia maculata)

GRACEFUL FLIER ►

A spotted longhorn beetle takes to the air. Like other insects, these beetles have two sets of flying muscles in their thorax (mid-body section). The hard front wings are held up to help steady the insect in flight. Most beetles are competent fliers, but they do not specialize in flying like some other insect species.

Focus on

1 When on the ground, the wing cases of the cockchafer beetle (*Melolontha melolontha*) meet over its body. The delicate rear wings are folded under the elytra and cannot be seen. Cockchafer beetles are also known as May bugs or June bugs, as it is in these months that they are usually seen.

Beetles, bugs and other insects are the only animals without a backbone that are able to fly. They take to the air to escape from their enemies and to move from place to place in search of food. Most beetles and bugs are expert fliers.

Bugs with two pairs of wings use both sets for flying. Their front and rear wings flap up and down together. The hardened front wings of a beetle are called elytra. They are not used for powering flight but steady the beetle as it flies. The long rear wings sweep up and down to power the beetle through the air.

2 A cardinal beetle (*Pyrochroa serraticornis*) prepares for take-off by raising its front wings out of the way and flexing its rear flight muscles. This process checks that the wings are in good working order and warms the beetle's muscles for the flight ahead. When the warm-up is finished, the beetle is ready to go.

3 A black-tipped soldier beetle (*Rhagonycha fulva*) positions itself for take-off like a plane taxiing down a runway. It finds a breezy spot by climbing a tall plant stem. Then it balances its body on top. In this exposed place, the wind may carry it away as it raises its wings. If not, the beetle will launch itself by leaping into the air.

Beetles in Flight

4 A cockchafer manoeuvres between plant stems. Its wing cases help to provide the lift it needs to remain airborne. Long rear wings provide flapping power to propel the beetle through the air. Cockchafers are clumsy fliers and sometimes stray into houses on dark evenings, drawn by the light. Indoors, the beetle may crash into objects in the unfamiliar setting, but it is so well protected that it is rarely hurt.

5 A freeze-frame photograph shows the flapping wing movements of a *Pectocera fortunei* beetle in mid-flight. These small, light beetles find it fairly easy to stay airborne. However, their small size is a disadvantage in windy conditions, when they are sometimes blown off course.

6 A cockchafer prepares to land on an oak leaf. The beetle's rear wings are angled downwards to help it lose height. As it comes in to land, the legs will move forward to take the beetle's weight on the leaf. The veins that strengthen the delicate rear wings can be clearly seen in this picture.

15

Senses

◄ SPINY SENSORS
Tanner beetles (*Prionus coriarius*)
have long, curving antennae.
The antennae are covered with
patterns of tiny hairs. Each
hair is attached to a nerve that
sends signals to the insect's brain
when the hair is moved.

Beetles and bugs have keen senses, but
they do not sense the world in the same
way that humans do. Most beetles and
bugs have good eyesight and a keen sense
of smell, but no sense of hearing. The main
sense organs are on the head.

Most beetles and bugs have two large
eyes, called compound eyes because they
are made up of many tiny lenses. These are
particularly good at sensing movement.
Some beetles and bugs also have simple,
bead-like eyes on top of their heads, which
are sensitive to light and dark.

The antennae are the main sense tools
for most beetles and bugs. They are used for
smelling and feeling, and in some species
for hearing and tasting, too. Antennae
come in various shapes — some beetles and
bugs have special feelers called palps on
their mouthparts.

Sensitive hairs all over the insects'
bodies pick up tiny currents in the air,
which may alert them to
enemies nearby.

▲ BRANCHING ANTENNAE
This unusual beetle from Central
America has branched antennae
that look like the antlers of a stag.
The branches are usually held closed,
but the insect can also fan them out
to pick up distant smells on the wind,
such as the scent of a faraway mate.
Smells such as these would be far
too faint for humans to detect.

SMELL AND TOUCH ►
Longhorn beetles (Cerambycidae) are named after their long
antennae. An insect's antennae are sometimes called its 'feelers'.
The term is rather misleading — the antennae *are* used for
feeling, but their main function is to pick up scents. Long antennae
like the longhorn beetle's are especially sensitive to smell and touch.

◄ ELBOW-SHAPED

The weevil's antennae are found on its long nose. Many weevils have jointed antennae, which bend in the middle like a human arm at the elbow. Some have special organs at the base of their antennae, which vibrate to sound and act as ears. This brush-snouted weevil (*Rhina tarbirostris*) has a bushy 'beard' of long, sensitive hairs on its snout.

COMPOUND EYES ►

The huge eyes of the harlequin beetle (*Acrocinus longimanus*) cover its head. Only the area from which its antennae sprout remains uncovered. Each compound eye is made up of hundreds of tiny lenses. Scientists believe that the signals from each lens build up to create one large picture. Even so, scientists are not sure what beetles and bugs see.

◄ TINY LENSES

A close-up of a beetle's compound eye shows that it is made up of many tiny facets, each of which points in a slightly different direction. Each is made up of a lens at the surface and a second lens inside. The lenses focus light down a central structure inside the eye, called the rhabdome, on to a bundle of nerves, which are behind the eye. These nerves then send messages to the brain. The hundreds of tiny lenses probably do not create the detailed, focused image produced by the human eye. However, they can pick up details and shapes and are very good at detecting tiny movements.

17

Plant-eaters and Pests

Beetles and bugs do not always eat the same food throughout their lives. Larvae often eat very different foods from their parents. Some adult beetles and bugs do not feed at all, and instead put all their energy into finding a mate and reproducing very quickly.

Most bugs and some beetles are herbivores. Different species feed on the leaves, buds, seeds and roots of plants, on tree wood or on fungi. Many plant-eaters become pests when they feed on cultivated plants or crops. Other beetles and bugs are carnivores, or recycle waste by consuming dead plants or animals. Others nibble things that humans would not consider edible, such as clothes, woollen carpets, wooden furniture and even animal dung.

▲ TUNNEL-EATERS
This tree has been eaten by bark beetles (Scolytidae). Females lay their eggs under tree bark. When the young hatch, each eats its way through the wood to create a long, narrow tunnel just wide enough to squeeze through.

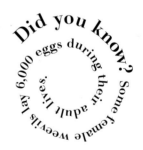

Did you know? Some female weevils lay 6,000 eggs during their adult lives.

Squash bug
(Coreus marginatus)

◄ SQUASH-LOVERS
Squash bugs are named after the food they like best. The squash-plant family includes courgettes (zucchini) and pumpkins. This bug is about to nibble a courgette flower bud. Most squash bugs are green or brown. They feed on the green parts of squash plants, and also on the seeds, which harms future crops. The insects are a pest in the USA.

▲ A PLAGUE OF APHIDS

Aphids are small, soft-bodied bugs. They use their sharp, beak-like mouths to pierce the stems of plants and suck out the sap inside. Aphids feed on the sap of plants, which is found in the stems and veins of leaves. These insects breed very quickly in warm weather.

▲ BEETLE ATTACK

Colorado beetles (*Leptinotarsa decemlineata*) are high on the list of dangerous insects in many countries. The beetles originally came from western USA, where they ate the leaves of local plants. When European settlers came and cultivated potatoes, the beetles ate the crop and did great damage. Colorado beetles later spread to become a major pest in Europe, but are now controlled by pesticides.

▲ SCALY FEEDERS

Most female scale insects (Coccoidae family) have neither legs nor wings, but they can be identified as bugs from the way their mouth is formed. Scale insects are usually well camouflaged, but the species shown here can be seen clearly. They are feeding on a juicy melon by piercing the skin and sucking up the sap.

▲ THE EVIL WEEVIL

These grains of wheat have been infested by grain weevils (*Sitophilus zeamais*). The adult weevils bore through the grain's hard case with their long snouts to reach the soft kernel inside. Females lay their eggs inside the kernels. Then, when the young hatch, they can feed in safety.

Scavengers and Hunters

Ground beetle
(*Lorica pilicornis*)

▲ **SPEEDY HUNTER**

A ground beetle feeds on a juicy worm it has caught. Ground beetles are a large family of beetles, with over 20,000 species. Many species cannot fly, hence their name. However, most ground beetles are fast runners. The beetle uses its speed to overtake its fleeing victim. Once trapped, the victim is firmly grabbed in the beetle's powerful jaws.

Many beetles and some bugs are carnivores (meat-eaters). Some hunt and kill live prey, others prefer their meat dead. Called scavengers, they feed on the remains of animals. Some other beetles and bugs are parasites that live on larger animals and eat their flesh, or drink their blood, without killing them.

Most predator beetles and bugs hunt fellow insects or other minibeasts such as millipedes. Some tackle larger game, such as fish, tadpoles, frogs, snails and worms. Beetles and bugs use a variety of different tricks and techniques to catch and overpower their prey. Most beetles seize their victims in their jaws, and crush or crunch them up to kill them. Bugs suck their victims' juices from their bodies while they are still alive.

◄ **GONE FISHING**

Great diving beetles (*Dytiscus marginalis*) are fierce aquatic hunters. They hunt down fish, tadpoles, newts and minibeasts that live in ponds and streams. This beetle has caught a stickleback. It grabs the fish in its jaws, then injects it with digestive juices that dissolve the fish's flesh. When the victim finally stops struggling and dies, the beetle begins to feed.

Famous Victim

Charles Darwin (1809–1882) was a British naturalist who first developed the theory of evolution – the idea that species develop over time to fit their environment. Darwin's theory was inspired by a trip to South America to study wildlife. On returning to Britain, Darwin fell victim to a mysterious illness, which weakened him for the rest of his life. Some historians believe that he was bitten by a South American assassin bug that carried a dangerous disease.

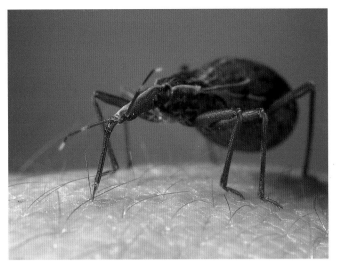

▲ VAMPIRE BEETLE

Most assassin bugs (Reduviidae family) are killers. Many species hunt minibeasts and suck their juices dry. Some are parasites. The species above feeds on humans by injecting their skin with a pain-killer so it can feast unnoticed.

EATEN ALIVE ▶

This shield bug *(Palomena prasina)* has caught a caterpillar. With a victim in its clutches, it uses its curving mouthparts to suck its prey dry. Most types of shield bugs are plant-eaters, but some hunt living creatures. The bugs use their front legs to hold their victims steady while they feast on them.

Did you know? Great diving beetles store air under their wings when they dive.

◀ NO ESCAPE

A snail-hunter beetle (*Calosoma*) tackles a small snail. To protect itself, the snail retreats into its shell and seals the opening with slime. In response, the beetle squirts a liquid into the shell to dissolve the slime and kill the snail.

Escaping Danger

The naturalist Charles Darwin's theory of evolution explains how only the fittest animals survive to breed and pass on their characteristics to the next generation. The key to survival is escaping danger. Beetles and bugs have many enemies in the natural world. They also have many ways of avoiding attack. Many species run, fly, hop or swim away, but some species are also armed with weapons. Some bugs and beetles can bite or use sharp spines for protection. Others are armed with poisonous fluids or taste nasty. These insects usually have bright patterns, which tells predators such as birds to stay away.

▲ **PROTECTIVE SPINES**
A weevil (*Lixus barbiger*) from the island of Madagascar has an impressive array of sharp spines on its back. Few predators will try such a prickly morsel – if they do, the pain may make them drop their meal!

▲ **READY TO SHOOT**
Desert skunk beetles (*Eleodes armata*) defend themselves by shooting a foul-smelling spray from their abdomens. This beetle has taken up a defensive posture by balancing on its head with its abdomen raised in the air. It is ready to fire its spray if an intruder comes close. Most predators will back away.

▼ **WHAT A STINK**
Squash bugs (*Coreus marginatus*) are also known as stink bugs because of the smelly spray they produce to ward off enemies. Like other insects, squash bugs do not actively *decide* to defend themselves. They instinctively react when their sense organs tell them that danger is near.

Blistering Attack

The blister beetles (Meloidae family) give off a chemical that causes human and animal skin to blister. Centuries ago, the chemical was thought to cure warts. Doctors applied blister beetles to the skin of patients suffering from the infection. The 'cure' was probably painful and did not work.

▼ TRICKY BEETLE

The devil's coach-horse beetle has several ways of defending itself from attack. First, it raises its tail in a pose that mimics a stinging scorpion (below). This action is a trick, for the beetle cannot sting. If the trick does not work, the beetle gives off an unpleasant smell to send its enemies reeling. If all else fails, it delivers a painful bite with its large jaws.

Devil's coach-horse beetle
(Staphylinus olens)

◄ PLAYING DEAD

This weevil from East Africa is trying to fool an enemy by playing dead. It drops to the ground and lies on its back with its legs curled in a lifeless position. This trick works well on enemies that eat only live prey. However, it does not work on the many predators that are not fussy whether their victims are alive or dead.

WARNING ENEMIES ►

The cardinal beetle's body contains chemicals that have a terrible taste to predators. The beetle's blood-red appearance helps to warn its enemies away. This will only work if the predator has tried to eat another beetle of the same species. If so, it will recognize the species by its appearance and leave it alone.

Cardinal beetle
(Pyrochroa coccinea)

Focus on

Ladybirds (also called ladybugs) are the only insects that many people will touch because they are known to be harmless. There are more than 4,000 different types of ladybirds in temperate and tropical countries all over the world. The insects are easy to recognize because of their rounded body shape. Most ladybirds are bright red, yellow or orange with black spots. This warns predators that ladybirds taste horrible.

Farmers and gardeners appreciate ladybirds because they are carnivores and feed on aphids and other minibeasts that cause damage to crops. One ladybird can eat up to 50 aphids a day. During the late 1800s, ladybirds were used to control the cottony cushion scale (*Icerya purchasi*) – a bug that threatened to destroy all the lemon trees in California, USA.

SPOTS OR STRIPES

The eyed ladybird (*Anatis ocellata*) is a large European species. Most ladybirds are red with black spots. Some have yellow or white spots, or a variety of markings, like this species (above). Some ladybirds have stripes instead of spots, and others are black with no markings at all.

HEADS OR TAILS?

A seven-spot ladybird (*Coccinella septempunctata*) scurries across a leaf. Like all ladybirds, its bright markings are found on the elytra (wing cases), which fold over the insect's back. The head and thorax are black. The pale markings that look like eyes are actually on the thorax.

Ladybirds

FLY AWAY HOME

A ladybird in flight shows that, like other beetles, the insect holds its wing cases out of the way when flying. In spring, ladybirds lay their eggs on plants infested with aphids. When the hungry young ladybird grubs hatch, they devour large quantities of the plant-eating pests.

HEAVEN-SENT HELPERS

A ladybird munches an aphid. Ladybirds are popular with market gardeners because they eat aphids and other insects that attack trees and crops. In medieval times, Europeans believed that ladybirds were sent by the Virgin Mary to help farmers – hence the name ladybird.

WINTER SLEEP

Ladybirds cluster on a twig in winter. They survive the cold by entering a deep sleep called hibernation. They hibernate together in large numbers, in sheds, cellars or under tree bark. Collectors use this period to harvest large quantities of the beetles to sell to suppliers and garden shops for pest control.

Natural Disguises

Many beetles and bugs have patterns on their bodies that disguise them in the natural world. Such disguises are called camouflage and hide the insects from their predators. Various species imitate natural objects, including sticks, grass, seeds, bark and thorns. Others are disguised as unpleasant objects, such as animal droppings, which predators avoid when looking for food.

Some beetles and bugs have another clever way of surviving – they mimic the appearance or shape of insects such as wasps and ants that are poisonous or can sting. Predators recognize and avoid the warning signs of the harmless imitators, mistaking them for the dangerous minibeasts.

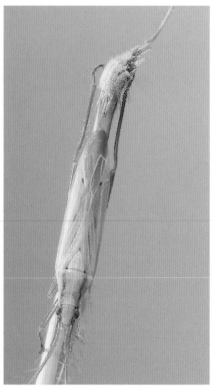

▲ BLADERUNNER
The top of this grass stem is actually a damsel bug (*Stenodema laengatum*) posing as a blade of grass. This bug's camouflage helps it to hide from its enemies – *and* sneak up on its prey, for the damsel bug is also a fierce predator.

Wasp beetle
(*Clytus arietis*)

▲ STRIPY WARNING
This beetle's bold black-and-yellow stripes suggest it is a wasp, armed with a painful sting. Although the insect is harmless, the black-and-yellow stripes are enough to put most predators off.

UNDER COVER ▶
A group of female scale insects (Coccoidae family) feed on a bay tree, disguised by their camouflage. The bugs also produce a nasty-tasting waxy white substance around their bodies. In this way, they can feed without being attacked by their enemies.

THORNY PROBLEM ▶

The sharp thorns on this twig look like part of the plant. They are, in fact, thorn bugs (*Umbonia crassicornus*). Each bug perfects its disguise by pointing in the same direction as the others on the twig. If they pointed in different directions, the bugs would look less like part of the plant. Even if a predator does spot the bugs, their prickly spines deter any passing enemy.

◀ **ANT COSTUME**

This treehopper (*Cyphonia clavata*) from the West Indies is a master of disguise. Its green body and transparent wings make it almost invisible when feeding upon leaves. In addition, it has an amazing black ant disguise on its back, which can be seen clearly by predators. True ants are armed with biting jaws and can also squirt stinging acid at their enemies. Predators will avoid them at all costs, and so the insect's clever disguise allows it to feed without being disturbed.

EYE SPY ▶

Click beetles have mottled patterns that help them to blend in with grass or tree bark. The eyed click beetle (*Alaus oculatus*, right) has two large eyespots on its thorax. These resemble the eyes of a large predator, such as an owl. These frightening markings will be enough to stop any predatory bird from attacking the beetle.

Focus on

At nightfall in warm countries, the darkness may be lit up by hundreds of tiny green-yellow lights. The lights are produced by insects called fireflies, also known as glow-worms. There are over 1,000 different types of fireflies, but not all species glow in the dark. The light is produced by special organs in the insects' abdomens. Fireflies are nocturnal (night-active) beetles. Some species produce a continuous greenish glow, others flash their lights on and off. These signals are all designed for one purpose – to attract a mate.

FIREFLY ANATOMY

Fireflies are flat and slender. Most are dark brown or black, with orange or yellow markings. The light organs are found in their abdomens. Most species have two sets of wings, but in some, the females have no wings at all.

PRODUCING LIGHT

A male firefly flashes his light to females nearby. He produces light when chemicals mix in his abdomen, causing a reaction that releases energy in the form of light. In deep oceans, many sea creatures produce light in a similar way, including fish and squid.

CODED SIGNALS

A female firefly climbs on to a grass stem to signal with her glowing tail. Each species of firefly has its own sequence of flashes, which serves as a private mating code. On warm summer evenings, the wingless females send this code to the flashing males that fly above.

Fireflies

FALSE CODE

Most adult fireflies feed on flower nectar or do not eat at all. However, the female of this North American species is a meat-eater – and her prey is other fireflies. When the flightless female sees a male firefly of a different species circling overhead, she flashes his response code to attract him to the ground. When he lands nearby, she pounces and eats him. She also flashes to males of her own species to attract them to her for mating.

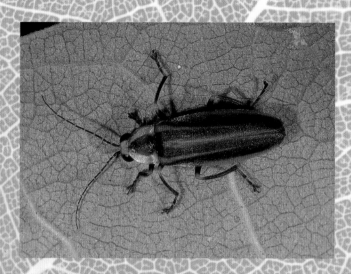

PULSE OF LIGHT

A group of fireflies light up a tree by a bridge as they signal to one another. In parts of Asia, some species of fireflies gather in large groups on trees. When one insect, called a pacemaker, flashes its light, all the other fireflies on the tree begin to flash their lights at the same time and to the same pattern. When this happens, the whole tree can be seen to glow and pulse with brilliant flashes of light.

YOUNG FIREFLIES

Like the adults, firefly larvae also make light. It is only the young, wingless insects and the flightless females that are called glow-worms. Young fireflies hatch from eggs laid in moist places by the females. Unlike most of their parents, all firefly larvae are meat-eaters. They kill slugs and snails by injecting them with poison. The young insects use their sharp jaws to hook the snails out of their shells and then gobble them up.

Attracting a Mate

One of the most important tasks for any animal is to continue its species by breeding. Beetles and bugs are no exception, and most must mate before they produce young.

Many beetles and bugs use scent to attract the opposite sex. They give off special smells that can travel a long distance through the air. The opposite sex then follow the trail of scent to find a partner to mate with. Some species use sound to attract a mate that is far away.

At close quarters, beetles and bugs may partly identify one another by sight. If two or more males are attracted to one female, the rivals may fight for the chance to mate. In some species, males and females spend several hours courting – checking that they have found a suitable mate. In other species, mating takes only a few minutes, after which the two insects go their separate ways.

▲ **IRRESISTIBLE SMELL**
Bark beetles (Scolytidae) live in tree trunks. Females of some species produce a scent, which male beetles pick up using their antennae. Sometimes, many males are drawn to just one female.

Did you know? Most beetles mate for only a few seconds but some mate for hours.

Rhododendron leafhopper
(*Graphocephala fennahi*)

◄ **SOUND SIGNALS**
Male leafhopper bugs 'sing' to attract their partners. They produce little squeaks and rasping sounds by rubbing their wings against their abdomen. The female insects have special hearing organs that can detect the high-pitched calls made by their mates. The sounds are far too quiet for humans to hear.

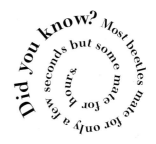

Ominous Sound

Deathwatch beetles (Xestobium rufovillosum) live in rotting logs and also in wooden buildings. During the breeding season, they tap on the wood at night to attract a mate. These sounds, sometimes heard by sick people awake at night, were once thought to be very unlucky. The tapping was believed to be an omen of death – hence the beetle's name.

▲ SPOTTING A MATE

Seven-spot ladybirds (*Coccinella septempunctata*), also known as ladybugs, mate on a leaf. The male mounts the female to release sperm to fertilize her eggs. They use sight to identify one another. They are guided to their own species by the different numbers of spots on their elytra (wing cases). Once they have found one of their own kind, they can mate successfully.

◄ FROG LEGS

This athletic-looking insect is a Malayan frog beetle. The species owes its name to the male beetle's powerful, frog-like hind legs. The insect uses his legs for leaping, but also for breeding. He clings on to the female beetle during mating, which helps to make sure that the union is fertile.

Malayan frog beetle
(*Sagra buqueti*)

▲ MALE AND FEMALE

A male aphid mates with a female. Many male and female beetles and bugs look similar to one another, but some aphids are different. The females have plump, green bodies. The males are thinner, with dark bodies and large wings. There are more female aphids than males. Males appear only in autumn, to mate with the females. The females lay fertilized eggs, which survive the winter and hatch in spring.

Focus on Stag

Courtship is a risky business for some types of beetles. Males will fight to mate with a female – sometimes to the death. Stag beetles (*Lucanus cervus*) are fighting beetles. They owe their name to the huge jaws of the male, which resemble a stag's antlers. The female stag beetle releases a scent which attracts males to her. Males can sense this scent up to 1km (half a mile) away. If two rival males appear, they may fight. Each beetle tries to hoist his rival in the air and smash him to the ground.

1 A male stag beetle displays his fearsome horns, which can be as long as his body. The beetle uses its jaws not for feeding, but to frighten away rival males and predators.

2 Like the male stag beetle, the body of the female is well protected. Her jaws are much smaller than the male's, however, and are not designed for fighting. The female's main purpose is to survive long enough to breed.

3 Two male beetles size each other up on the prime breeding ground of an old tree stump. Each male tries to frighten the other with his giant horns. If neither beetle backs down and scuttles away, the fight will start.

Beetle Contests

4 The rival males begin to wrestle. As they lock horns, each tries to gain the upper hand by gripping his enemy. The fierce-looking jaws rarely do serious damage, but the fight tests the strength and endurance of both insects.

5 The strongest beetle grips his enemy in his jaws and lifts him high. The other beetle is helpless in this position, but the victor struggles to keep his balance. One slip and the other beetle could take control.

6 The victorious beetle ends the contest by dashing his rival to the ground, or by throwing him off the log. If the loser lands on his back, he may be unable to get up – particularly if he is wounded. The defeated beetle may well be eaten alive by predatory insects, such as ants. The strongest male wins his right to mate with the female, and so pass on his characteristics to the next generation. This process ensures that only the strongest genes are passed on, guaranteeing the survival of the fittest.

The Life Cycle of Beetles

Beetles and bugs have different life cycles. During their lives, beetles pass through four stages. From eggs, they hatch into larvae (young) called grubs. The grubs do not look like their parents. Some have legs, but many look like long, pale worms. They all live in different places from the adults and eat different food.

Beetle larvae are hungry feeders. They feed, grow and shed their skins several times, but do not change form or grow wings. When the larva is fully grown, it develops a hard case and enters a resting stage, called a pupa. Inside the case, the grub's body is totally dissolved and then rebuilt. It emerges from its pupa as a winged adult. This amazing process is called complete metamorphosis. The word 'metamorphosis' means transformation.

▲ LAYING EGGS

A female cardinal beetle (*Pyrochroa coccinea*) lays its eggs in dead wood. The hard tip of the beetle's abdomen pierces the wood to lay the eggs inside. When the eggs hatch, the log provides the larvae with a hiding place from predators. They feast on the timber until they are fully grown.

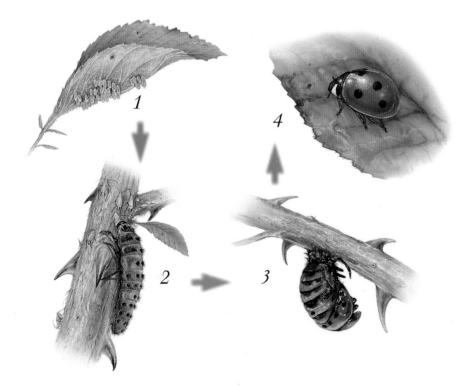

◀ THE FOUR STAGES

There are four stages in a beetle's life cycle. It begins life as an egg (1), then becomes a larva or grub (2). The full-grown larva then becomes a pupa (3) before it reaches adulthood (4). At each stage, the beetle's appearance is almost totally different from the last stage. In a way, a developing beetle is several animals in one. When the beetle finally emerges from its pupa as an adult, it is ready to breed, and so the life cycle can begin again.

◄ BEETLE EGGS

The female ladybird glues her eggs on to leaves so that they stand on end. Beetle eggs are generally rounded or oval. They are usually yellow, green or black for camouflage. Most eggs are laid in spring or summer, and most hatch between one week and one month later. Some eggs are laid in autumn and hatch the following spring. They take longer to hatch because of the cooler conditions.

LARVA ►

This cockchafer larva (*Melolontha melolontha*) looks nothing like the adult. Its long, fat body is very different from the adult's rounded shape. However, unlike many beetle grubs, it does have legs. The larva has no compound eyes or long antennae. Nor does it have wings, but moves about by wriggling its way through the soil.

◄ PUPA

When a beetle grub is fully grown, it attaches itself to a plant stem or hides underground. Then it develops a hard outer case to become a pupa. Unlike the grub, the pupa doesn't feed or move much. It looks dead, but inside its hard case, an amazing change is taking place. The insect's body breaks down into a kind of soup, and is reshaped into an adult beetle.

ADULT FORM ►

An adult seven-spot ladybird (*Coccinella septempunctata*) struggles out of its pupa case. It emerges complete with long, jointed legs, wings and antennae. Its yellow wing cases will develop spots after just a few hours. Some beetles spend only a week as pupae before emerging as fully grown adults. Others pass the whole winter in the resting stage, waiting to emerge until the following spring.

The Life Cycle of Bugs

Bugs develop in a different way from beetles. Most bugs hatch from eggs laid by females after mating. Newly hatched bugs are called nymphs and look like tiny adults, but they are wingless. Nymphs often eat the same food and live in the same places as their parents.

Unlike human skin, an insect's exoskeleton is not stretchy. Nymphs are hungry eaters, and as they feed and grow, their hard skins become too tight and must be shed several times. The nymphs then develop new skins, inside which there is space to grow. As they grow, they gradually sprout wings. After they shed their skin for the final time, the bugs emerge as winged adults. This process is called incomplete metamorphosis because, unlike beetles, bugs do not go through the pupa stage and totally rebuild their bodies.

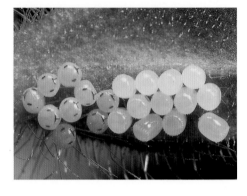

▲ BUG EGGS
Like other young insects, most bugs start out as eggs. These little yellow balls are shield bug eggs (*Eysarcoris fabricii*). They are all at various stages of development. The yellow eggs on the left are more developed than the paler eggs on the right, and will soon hatch into young.

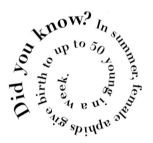

Did you know? In summer, female aphids give birth to up to 50 young in a week.

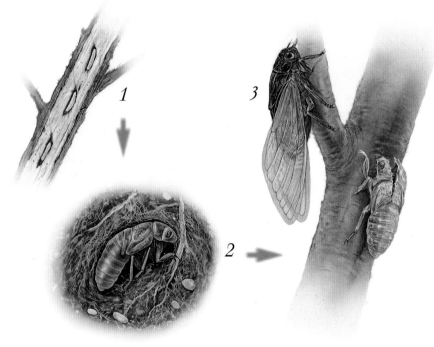

◄ THE THREE STAGES
There are three different stages in a bug's life. The first stage is the egg (1), from which the bug hatches as a nymph (2). The nymph gradually grows and sheds its skin a number of times. Each time it sheds it becomes more like an adult. The wing buds appear, and gradually lengthen as the nymph reaches adulthood (3).

EASY TARGET ▶

This young shield bug looks like its parents, but it is wingless and cannot fly. After shedding its skin, the nymph has no hard skin to protect it and is extremely vulnerable. At this stage, young bugs are 'sitting ducks,' and many fall victim to predators such as lizards and birds. The new exoskeleton hardens within just a few hours. With luck, this new layer will protect the young bug for long enough to reach adulthood.

◀ FOAMY HIDEOUT

Some nymphs have special ways of avoiding predators. This froghopper nymph (*Philaemus spumarius*) hides inside the unpleasant-looking foam behind it, known as 'cuckoo spit'. The bug produces the froth itself by giving off a sticky liquid, which it blows into a foam. The cuckoo spit makes a good hiding place from predators, and also screens the bug from the sun.

YOUNG HUNTER ▶

Just a few hours after hatching, a young pond skater (*Gerris najas*, right) begins to live and feed on the water's surface, just like its parents. A pond skater's feet are covered in dense water-repellent hair, which allows it to walk on the surface of the water. Pond skaters are expert predators, catching other water creatures and then feeding by sucking out the victims' juices with their long feeding tubes.

◀ BREEDING WITHOUT MALES

In autumn, male and female aphids breed and lay eggs in the normal way. In summer, however, female aphids can reproduce without males, and give birth to live offspring without mating or even laying eggs. This aphid (left) is giving birth to a fully formed young. This amazing process is called parthenogenesis (meaning virgin birth.) The babies grow up quickly, and can themselves breed after just one week.

▲ SOIL DWELLERS

Click beetle larvae (Elateridae family) are called wireworms. They have worm-like bodies and tiny legs. Most are bright yellow or orange. Wireworms live in soil and feed on the roots of grasses. They can cause damage to crops by eating their roots.

▲ LIVELY LARVA

A ladybird larva (*Coccinella septempunctata*) munches aphids. Many grubs are legless or not quick on their feet, but young ladybirds are nimble and lively, like tiny lizards.

UNDER DUNG ▶

Beetles that live above ground need to find some way to protect themselves from enemies. This green tortoise beetle larva (*Cassida viridis*) is hiding from predators by carrying a lump of dung on its tail.

Young Beetles

The main purpose of an adult beetle is to reproduce. The goal for a larva is to reach adulthood, which it does by feeding, growing and avoiding predators. Most beetles lay their eggs on or near a suitable food source for their young, such as dead wood, plants or even in a living animal.

Various species of beetles spend different amounts of time as eggs, larvae, pupae and adults. Ladybirds, also known as ladybugs, spend one week as an egg, three to six weeks as larvae and then another week as pupae. Stag beetles take longer to grow. They hatch after two weeks as an egg, then spend up to five years as grubs living in dead wood and another eight months as pupae. Adult stag beetles live only a few months before they die.

▲ WOODBORERS

Metallic woodboring beetles (*Buprestidae* family)
live in tunnels in dead wood. The larvae feed on
the timber, but it is not very nourishing. So the
young grubs must spend many years feeding
before they are ready to pupate and become
adults. One type of woodboring beetle spends
40 years in the timber before it is fully grown.

Deadly Beetle

*The pupae of a particular kind of South
African leaf beetle produce a deadly poison.
Just the smallest trace of the poison can kill
a large animal, such as a gazelle. Kalahari
bushmen tip the points of their arrows with
the beetle's poison before going on hunting
trips. Preparing their weapons is very
dangerous. The hunters take great care to
make sure that the poison does not get into
cuts or grazes on their own skin. If it does,
they could die.*

▲ HIDDEN TRAP

The tiger beetle larva (*Cicindela* species) is a stealthy
predator. It makes a burrow in the soil and fills the
entrance with its huge jaws. It then waits until a passing
insect comes close enough to grab. The beetle's jaws snap
shut and it drags its prey into its burrow to finish it off.

FREE AT LAST ▶

A nut weevil larva (*Curculio nucum*) pokes its head out of a
hazel nut. Its mother drilled into the nut to lay her egg inside.
The grub hatched and fed inside the nut, then gnawed its
way to freedom. It will not spend long in the open
air. Instead, it will quickly burrow into the
soil, where it will pupate.

Caring for the Young

Oak roller weevil
(*Attelebus nitens*)

Most beetles and bugs do not actively care for their offspring. They simply lay their eggs on a suitable food source, and then leave the young to fend for themselves. A few species, though, are caring parents. Some beetles, such as oak roller weevils, take great effort to protect their eggs. Other species, such as burying beetles, feed their larvae themselves.

Cross-winged bugs, such as shield bugs, guard and watch over their nymphs until the babies become big enough to look after themselves. Passalid beetles take even greater care of their young. Like ants, termites, and some bees and wasps, they are social insects. Social insects live and work together in a group. These beetle parents, and even their older offspring, take great pains to rear their young.

▲ SAFE HOME
Oak roller weevils lay their eggs high up in oak trees. The females use their jaws to snip the oak leaves into sections. They then curl the leaves into tight rolls, in which they lay their eggs. Inside the rolls, the eggs are safe from predators that might eat the eggs or feed them to their own young.

Did you know? Some water beetles weave a web around the eggs to keep them dry.

CARING PARENT ▶
A female shield bug, known as the parent bug (*Elasmucha grisea*), protects her young from a predatory spider. Her large brood of nymphs cluster behind her for safety. A distant relative, the male giant water bug, protects his eggs by carrying them on his body until they hatch.

Sacred Scarabs

Scarab beetles were sacred to the ancient Egyptians. They symbolized the sun-god, Ra. Each day, Ra rolled the fiery ball of the sun across the sky, just as the scarab beetle rolls a ball of dung to a suitable place to lay its eggs. The scarab beetle was a symbol of rebirth, and it was used to decorate tombs and many sacred objects.

◀ **DUNG-ROLLERS**

Dung beetles are part of the scarab beetle family (Scarabaeidae). These beetles and their young feed on the droppings of mammals such as buffalo. To provide for the young, the male and female beetles shape the dung into a ball. They then roll it to a safe place, where they bury it. The female beetle lays her eggs in the dung ball. When the young hatch, they will have a ready food supply in a safe hiding hole. The buried dung also helps to fertilize the soil.

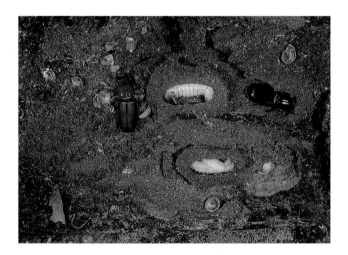

▲ **FAMILY GROUPS**

Passalid beetles live in families. They inhabit rotting tree trunks, in a maze of tunnels. These parent beetles are tending pupae in their white cocoons. When the pupae emerge as adults, they stay in the nest to help rear the next generation of young.

▲ **PERSONAL CARE**

A burying beetle (*Nicrophorus humator*) crawls over a dead shrew. The parent beetles tunnel under the dead body to bury it. The female then lays her eggs on the animal. Some beetles wait for the young to hatch, then feed them the meat of the dead mammal themselves.

41

Homes and Habitats

Around the world, beetles and bugs are found in all sorts of different habitats. Most live in hot, tropical regions or in mild, temperate areas. Many beetles and bugs are found in places that have moderate or heavy rainfall, but some tough species manage to live in deserts. Others can survive on snow-capped mountains or frozen icefields, in caves, sewers and even hot springs.

Beetles and bugs that live in very cold or very hot places must be able to cope with extreme temperatures. Many survive the harsh weather as pupae, or as eggs in the soil. In deserts, most species are active at night, when the air is cooler. The toughest species can go for long periods without food or even water. These insects are small enough to shelter from storms or predators in tiny nooks and crannies.

▲ PARASITES
Bedbugs (*Cimex lectularius*) are parasites that live and feed on warm-blooded animals. Some species suck human blood. Bedbugs that infest birds and furry mammals live in their nests, or among their feathers or hair. Kept warm by their host animal, some bedbugs can even survive in cold places such as the Arctic.

Did you know? Water boatmen can fly many kilometres to find a new home.

◄ UPSIDE-DOWN WORLD
Water boatmen (*Notonecta maculata*) live upside-down in water. The bug hangs just below the water surface, and uses its oar-like legs to move about, rather like rowing. Like many bugs that live in water, the boatman is a hunter. It grabs minibeasts that have fallen into the water, and sucks their juices dry.

LONG LIMBS ▶

This stilt-legged bug (*Berytidae* family) lives in caves in the Caribbean. Its long, thin legs and antennae help it to feel its way in the dark. The legs and antennae are also covered with hairs that can detect the slightest air currents, alerting the bug to the presence of other animals.

◀ DESERT SURVIVOR

The fog-basking beetle (*Onymachris unguicularis*) lives in the Namib Desert, in southern Africa. This beetle has an ingenious way of drinking. When fog and mist swirl over the dunes, it does a handstand and points its abdomen in the air. Moisture gathers on its body, then trickles down special grooves on its back into its waiting mouth.

SURVIVING IN CAVES ▶

This beetle (*Aphaenops* species) lives in caves high in the Pyrenees Mountains, between France and Spain. Its body is not well camouflaged, but in the dark of the caves, disguise is not important. Scientists believe some cave-dwelling species developed from beetles that first lived in the caves during the last Ice Age, about a million years ago.

◀ DUNE DWELLER

The dune beetle (*Onymacris bicolor*) lives in the deserts of southern Africa. It is one of the few white beetles. White reflects the rays of the sun and helps to keep the insect cool. The pale appearance blends in well with the sand where it lives, which helps it to hide from predators. The beetle's elytra (wing cases) are hard and close-fitting, and so help to conserve (keep) precious body moisture in this dry region. Long legs raise the beetle's body above the burning desert sand.

Tropical Beetles and Bugs

An amazing range of beetles and bugs live in tropical countries, where the weather is always hot. In this climate, these cold-blooded insects can stay active all year round. Parts of the tropics have dense rainforests and this wealth of plant food means that rainforests contain more types of beetles and bugs than any other habitat on Earth. A single rainforest tree may hold several thousand different kinds of insects. Some beetles and bugs live high in the treetops. Others live among the tangled vegetation halfway up tall trees, or among the decaying plants and fungi of the forest floor.

The tropical regions are home to many brightly marked beetles and bugs. Other species have subtle patterns that blend in with their home.

▲ BRIGHT BUG

Tropical shield bugs (Heteroptera order) come in many bright patterns. Some are to warn enemies, which tell predators that these insects can defend themselves. This shield bug nymph from Indonesian can also produce a foul smell if attacked.

Did you know? Cicadas that live in moist places coat their bodies with a waterproof wax.

◄ UNDER COVER

Most jewel beetles and bugs are known for their bright, rainbow patterns, but this species (Buprestidae family) from southern Africa is more subtly marked. The hairs on the beetle's thorax add to its disguise, and may help repel attackers. Its bright, shiny relatives are often prized by collectors. Sometimes these unfortunate bugs are actually made into ornaments.

◄ BEAUTIFUL BEETLE

Tropical rainforests are home to some of the world's most spectacular beetles. Few are more splendid than this golden beetle from Central America. Surprisingly, the beetle's shiny skin works as camouflage. The insect looks like a raindrop glinting in the sun, so its enemies don't notice it. The effect is created when sunlight bounces off the insect's skin.

LURKING HUNTER ►

This assassin bug (Reduviidae) is from Africa. Like most of its family, it lies in wait for minibeasts, then sucks its victims dry. The bug can be seen clearly on a dark leaf, but it is well camouflaged in the tropical flowers and stems among which it hides. The eyespots on its back scare away enemies.

◄ CLOWN BUG

A harlequin bug from southern Africa rests on a tree seed. These bugs are named after clowns called harlequins, who wear costumes with bright patterns. In Australia, male, female and young harlequins are all brilliantly patterned with red, yellow or blue with green spots. Some harlequin species make their homes high in the treetops.

BARK MIMIC ►

A longhorn beetle (Cerambycidae family) from south-west Africa demonstrates the power of camouflage. The beetle's feelers and its square shape resemble the cracks and flaking texture of the tree bark, making it almost invisible. Its long antennae are spread wide to pick up scents in the wind.

Focus on

Cicadas are sometimes called locusts or harvest flies, but they are neither. These insects are bugs that live in the tropics and warm countries. They are well known for their noisy 'songs', which the males produce to attract a mate.

Like other bugs, cicadas undergo incomplete metamorphosis to become adults. Some species live longer than most other insects — periodical cicadas can be 17 years old before they reach adulthood. The bugs survive beneath the ground by gnawing on plant roots.

BIG BUG
Most cicadas are large insects and can be more than 4cm (1½in) long. This giant cicada from Africa is even bigger and has a wingspan of 15cm (6in).

RED EYE
This cicada from Australia is sucking plant sap. Its long, straw-like mouthparts pierce the plant stem. It has large red eyes — hence its name, red-eye cicada (*Psaltodea moerens*).

SINGING FOR A MATE
Male cicadas sing 'courtship songs' to attract the females. When the male flexes muscles in his abdomen, two thin, drum-like sheets of skin on the sides of the abdomen vibrate to make a stream of clicking sounds.

Cicadas

LAYING EGGS

After mating, the female cicada lays her eggs on a twig. She uses the sharp tip of the egg-layer on her abdomen to cut slits in the bark for hundreds of tiny eggs. The nymphs hatch about six weeks later. They drop to the ground and burrow into the soil to develop.

SHEDDING SKIN

When the cicada nymph is fully grown, it climbs out of the soil and clambers up a tree trunk to shed its skin one last time. This is an amazing sight. The back of the cicada's old skin bursts apart, and the young adult slowly struggles out. This bug is a dog-day cicada (*Canicularis* species), a species from North America. While it does not live quite as long as the periodical cicada, this nymph spends up to seven years underground before becoming an adult.

SPREAD YOUR WINGS

As the dog-day cicada scrambles clear of its old skin, its wings uncurl and lengthen. The bug spreads its wings out to dry. Until it can fly, it is an easy target for birds and lizards. The young adults fly off to sing for a few weeks before they die. During their brief adult lives, they will mate and lay eggs, so that a new generation of bugs will emerge from the soil.

Temperate Beetles and Bugs

The world's temperate regions lie north and south of the tropics. Temperate lands have a mild climate, with warm summers and cold winters. When trees and plants lose their leaves in winter, food is scarce for beetles and bugs, and many adult insects die. Their eggs or pupae survive to hatch in the spring. The natural vegetation of temperate regions is grassland or woodland. These rich food sources ensure that temperate lands are home to thousands of beetle and bug species.

Green shield bug
(Palomena prasina)

▲ **SPITTING BLOOD**

Bloody-nosed beetles (*Timarcha tenebricosa*) are large, slow-moving insects. Their striking black appearance can attract unwelcome attention. To protect itself, this beetle has a secret weapon – it can spurt a bright red liquid from its mouth. Most predators will leave the beetle alone if faced with this sight.

▲ **GREEN SHIELD BUG**

This shield bug lives on trees and shrubs. In the spring and summer it is bright green, but in autumn it turns reddish brown, like the leaves it lives on. The shield bug hibernates during the winter. When it re-emerges in the spring, the bright green will have returned. There are a number of types of shield bug. The gorse shield bug (*Piezodorus lituratus*) is red only as a young adult. After hibernation, it becomes yellow-green.

◄ CLEVER CLICK

Click beetles get their name from the clicking sound they make. The beetle hooks its thorax together by locking a peg into a hole on its belly. When the peg is released with a click, it throws the beetle into the air, helping it to escape from enemies. The beetle also uses the click mechanism to right itself if it falls on its back.

Hairy click beetle
(Athous hirtus)

WILD ROVER ►

Rove beetles (Staphylinidae family) are a large beetle family, with more than 20,000 species. They are found in tropical and temperate lands worldwide. With their long, slim bodies, some species look like earwigs. Others are very hairy. Most species lurk under stones or in the soil.

Rove beetle
(Creophilus maxillosus)

◄ INSECT PARTNERS

Aphids produce a sweet liquid called honeydew – a popular food of many ants. These ants are collecting honeydew from aphids on a foxglove. Some types of ants keep aphids in the same way that people keep cattle. They 'milk' the aphids by stroking them with their antennae. This makes the aphids release their honeydew. In return, the ants protect the aphids from ladybirds (also known as ladybugs), and sting the aphids' enemies if they attack.

CANNIBAL CARDINALS ►

The cardinal beetle is recognizable by its distinctive, bright red elytra (wing cases). Adults are usually found on flowering shrubs or tree trunks. The females lay their eggs under the dry bark of trees. When the eggs grow into larvae, they eat other insects that live in the tree. If the larvae cannot find food, they feed upon each other.

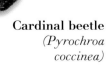

Cardinal beetle
(Pyrochroa coccinea)

49

Focus on Living

Some beetles and bugs live in and on fresh water – not only ponds and rivers but also icy lakes, mountain streams, muddy pools and stagnant marshes. Most of the larvae live in the water, where rich stocks of food make good nurseries.

Different types of beetles and bugs live at different depths in the water. Some live on the water surface or just below it. Other species swim in the mid-depths, or lurk in the mud or sand at the bottom. Beetles and bugs that live underwater carry a supply of air down with them so that they can breathe.

SURFACE SPINNERS

Whirligig beetles (*Gyrinus natator*) are oval, flattened beetles that live on the surface of ponds and streams. Their compound eyes are divided into two halves, designed to see above and below the water. When swimming, they move in circles, like spinning toys called whirligigs.

SKATING ON WATER

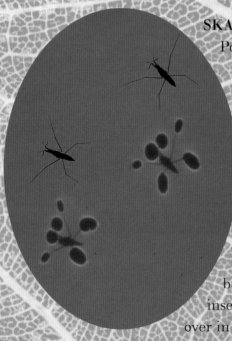

Pond skaters (*Gerris lacustris*) live on the water's surface. They move about like ice skaters, buoyed up by their light bodies. The bugs' legs make dimples on the surface of the water, but do not break it. When these bugs sense a drowning insect nearby, they skate over in gangs to feed on it.

SPINY STRAW

Water scorpions have long spines on their abdomens like true scorpions. The spines have no sting, but are used to suck air from the surface. Sensors on the spine tell the bug when it is too deep to breathe.

in *Water*

THE SCORPION STRIKES

Water scorpions (*Nepa cinerea*) are fierce predators. This bug has seized a stickleback fish in its pincer-like front legs. It then uses its mouthparts to pierce the fish's skin and suck its juices dry. Compared to some aquatic insects, water scorpions are not strong swimmers. They sometimes move about underwater by walking along water plants.

AIR SUPPLY

Saucer bugs (*Ilyacoris*) are expert divers. In order to breathe, the bug takes in air through spiracles (holes) in its body. Tiny bubbles of air are also trapped between the bug's body hairs, giving it its silvery appearance. Saucer bugs use their front legs to grab their prey. They cannot fly, but move from pond to pond by crawling through the grass.

DIVING DOWN

You can often see water boatmen (*Corixa punctata*) just below the water surface, but they can also dive below. They use their back legs to row underwater, and breathe air trapped under their wings. The females lay their eggs on water plants or glue them to stones on the stream bed. The eggs hatch two months later.

Other Insects

Many species of insects are thought of as beetles or bugs. They may look similar or have similar habits, but scientists think they are different enough to put them in a separate order. For example, true flies (Diptera) go through a complete metamorphosis, just like beetles. However, they only have one pair of wings, instead of two.

Over the next few pages we look at some of the other orders of insects and investigate the characteristics that make them unique.

There are some features that all insects share. All insects have a head, a thorax and an abdomen, and three pairs of legs. They have antennae and compound eyes. Almost all insects hatch from eggs.

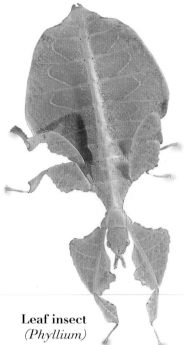

Leaf insect
(*Phyllium*)

▲ STICK AND LEAF INSECTS

Leaf insects resemble leaves or bark. Stick insects, which belong to the same order, look like twigs with their long, thin legs and bodies.

INSECT ORDERS ▶

This illustration shows 20 of the major insect orders, with each order represented by a particular insect. Some scientists have identified less than 25 orders, some more than 30. Some orders contain several familiar insects.

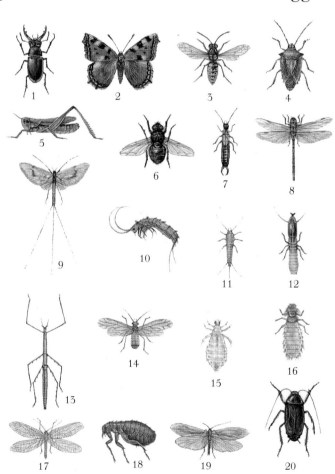

1. Coleoptera: beetle
2. Lepidoptera: butterfly
3. Hymenoptera: wasp
4. Hemiptera: shield bug
5. Orthoptera: grasshopper
6. Diptera: fly
7. Dermaptera: earwig
8. Odonata: dragonfly
9. Ephemeroptera: mayfly
10. Collembola: springtail

11. Thysanura: silverfish
12. Isoptera: termite
13. Phasmida: stick insect
14. Psocoptera: bark lice
15. Anoplura: sucking lice
16. Mallophaga: biting lice
17. Neuroptera: lacewing
18. Siphonaptera: flea
19. Trichoptera: caddisfly
20. Dictyoptera: cockroach

◄ CADDISFLIES

This strange creature is a caddisfly larva. It belongs to the Trichoptera order, which means 'hair wings'. The adults have two pairs of hairy, flimsy wings and look similar to moths. Their larvae grow up in ponds and streams, protected by silk cocoons and camouflaged with sticks and stones. The caddisfly larva undergoes a complete metamorphosis to become an adult.

COCKROACHES ►

Cockroaches belong to the order Dictyoptera, which means 'net wings'. They live in forests, caves and people's homes. Cockroaches hide by day and come out at night to feed. Once inside a house, it can be difficult to get rid of them.

Did you know? Some female earwigs lick their eggs to keep them free of infection.

Earwig
(*Forficula auriculariam*)

◄ EARWIGS

The Dermaptera order, which means 'skin wings', includes earwigs (left). These insects' abdomens end in a pair of long, fierce pincers. Their young hatch as nymphs. Insects in the Dermaptera order have slim, brown bodies and two pairs of wings. Their long rear wings are usually folded under their short, leathery, skin-like front wings, which have earned them their name.

LICE ►

Lice are parasitic insects that live on birds and mammals. They make up several orders, including biting (Mallophaga) and sucking (Anoplura) lice. All are wingless. Head lice, shown here, are sucking lice. They live and lay their eggs, called nits, in human hair.

True Flies

After beetles, flies are one of the largest insect orders. Over 90,000 different kinds of fly have been identified, including gnats, midges and mosquitoes. These hardy insects live almost everywhere on Earth, including the icy polar regions. Unlike beetles and bugs, flies have only one pair of wings. This is reflected in their order name, Diptera, which means 'two wings'. All that remains of the fly's hind wings are two little organs called halteres. These help the fly to balance and steer as it flies.

Ever unpopular, flies are considered dirty and carry diseases that can infect our food. Flies do have their uses, however. They fertilize flowers, and feed on dung and dead animals, reducing this waste around the world.

▲ FLY FOOD
This house fly is feeding on a piece of jelly. Taste sensors on its feet help it to detect its food. Like many kinds of flies, houseflies have mouths that work like sponges. They suck, or lick up, liquid foods such as sap and fruit juice. Some flies even feed on dung, rotting meat or blood.

Did you know? Over 10,000 species of craneflies are known to exist worldwide.

House fly
(Musca domestica)

INSECT ACROBATS ▶
This house fly is walking upside-down across the ceiling. Many flies have hooks and sticky pads on their feet, which help them to grip smooth surfaces. Their halteres (balancing organs) make them acrobatic fliers. They can hover, fly backwards and even land upside-down. Such skills help them to dodge fly-swatters.

▲ THIN AND FAT

Flies come in different shapes and sizes. Crane flies (Tipulidae family) such as the one above, are slim and delicate. Bluebottles and house flies are stout and chunky. Some flies are 0.5mm (¹⁄₃₂in) long – tinier than a pinhead. Others can measure a hundred times that size.

The Fly

This picture is taken from the horror film The Fly. *In the film, a scientist turns into a fly after an experiment goes wrong. Gruesome special effects make the film particularly scary. The theme proved so popular with audiences that several different versions have been made.*

▲ FOUR-STEP LIVES

Young flies are known as maggots. Like beetles, flies have four stages in their life cycle. They begin life as eggs, laid by the females in water, rotting plants or meat, or on animals. The eggs hatch into legless maggots (grubs). Later the maggots pupate to become adult flies.

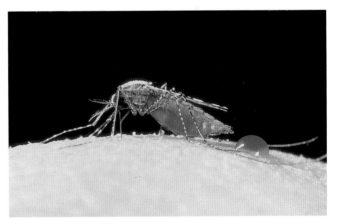

▲ CARRYING DISEASES

Mosquitoes (Culicdae) suck human and animal blood. This one is feeding from a human being. Using its needle-like mouthparts, the mosquito pierces its victim's skin to suck up blood. These insects can infect their prey with deadly diseases, including malaria and yellow fever.

Dragonflies

The order Odonata contains dragonflies and damselflies. It is a small order with just 5,000 species in total. Dragonflies and damselflies are found in wetlands worldwide, both tropical and temperate. Odonata means 'toothed' and refers to their sharp, pointed jaws. Dragonflies are large, slender insects. Their relatives, damselflies, are smaller and more delicate. Both dragonflies and damselflies come in many bright patterns including scarlet, blue and green.

Like bugs, dragonflies undergo incomplete metamorphosis, hatching as nymphs and gradually become more like adults. Both nymphs and adults are carnivores and expert hunters, but adults and young live in very different ways. Nymphs grow up underwater in ponds and streams. Adults are one of the largest winged insects and are powerful fliers.

▲ LARGE EYES

Dragonflies have extremely large compound eyes, as this close-up shows. The eyes cover most of the insect's head and almost meet at the top. Each compound eye has up to 30,000 lenses, each of which may help to build up a detailed picture. Dragonflies can detect movement easily and use their keen sight to track down their prey.

◄ FLYING CHAMP

Dragonflies are among the fastest insect fliers. They can race along at speeds of up to 95kph (60mph). Unlike other insects, their wings move independently. As each wing circles, it makes a figure of eight. This helps the insect to accelerate, brake and hover in one place – and also to steer with great accuracy.

Dragonfly
(Trithemis annulata)

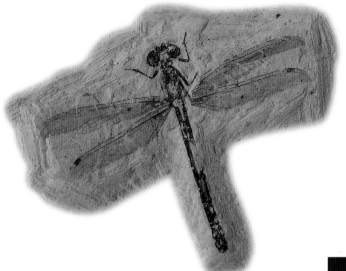

◄ ANCIENT INSECTS

Dragonflies are an ancient group of insects. From fossils, scientists have discovered that they flew on Earth 300 million years ago. They existed before the age of the dinosaurs. Some prehistoric dragonflies were giant insects, with wings that measured up to 60cm (2ft) across. No known modern species comes close to that size.

NIFTY HUNTER ►

A dragonfly feeds on a fly. It uses its sharp, pointed jaws to tear its prey into tiny chunks. Dragonflies often hunt in flight. They hold their spindly legs in front to form a small catching basket. Any flying insects within reach are quickly bagged. The dragonfly will sometimes even consume its prey in mid-flight.

◄ GROWING UP

Clinging to a plant stem, a young damselfly by a pond, emerges from shedding its skin the final time. Both dragonflies and damselflies lay their eggs in fresh water. The young hunt, feed and grow underwater. Gills on their abdomens allow them to extract oxygen from the water like fish. When fully grown, the nymph crawls up a plant stem and then sheds for the last time. As its skin splits, the young adult climbs out.

DRYING OUT ►

A young dragonfly rests after emerging from its shedded its skin. Its short, crumpled wings and abdomen gradually lengthen and harden as blood is pumped into them. Its patterns will appear soon. Adult dragonflies live only a few weeks, during which time they will mate and lay eggs.

Fleas, Grasshoppers and Mantids

Most beetles and bugs rely on the power of flight, but these three orders of insects have evolved different methods of moving around. Fleas are tiny, wingless parasites. Their strong muscles make them champion leapers. Fleas live on warm-blooded mammals and birds, and drink their blood. They belong to the order Siphonaptera, which refers to their sucking mouthparts and lack of wings.

Grasshoppers are also powerful leapers, well known for the loud, chirping noises they sing to attract a mate. These insects belong to the order Orthoptera, which means 'straight wings'. The grasshopper family includes crickets and locusts. Most grasshoppers are plant-eaters.

Mantids belong to the order Dictyoptera, and all are carnivores. These large insects are disguised to blend in with their surroundings. This superb camouflage helps them catch their prey. Unlike grasshoppers and fleas, mantids are found mainly in warm countries.

▲ HIGH JUMP CHAMPION

With no wings, fleas cannot fly. They are, however, amazing leapers. A flea can jump 30cm (12in) high – 130 times its own height. If humans could leap as high as fleas, we would be able to jump over tall buildings! The incredible leaping ability of a flea allows it to hop on to much larger animals as they pass by.

DEADLY PEST ▶

A rat flea (right) feeds on human blood. Different species of fleas are designed to feed on certain types of animals. If hungry, however, a flea will suck any animal's blood. By feeding from various hosts (victims), fleas pass on diseases. In medieval times, they carried a terrible disease called bubonic plague. Known as the Black Death, it killed half the population of Europe. The fleas carried the disease after biting infected rats.

SPINY LEGS ▶

This close-up of a mantis shows the insect's spiny front legs. It uses its forelegs to capture insects, which it then eats alive. The mantis lurks among flowers or leaves, waiting for passing insects. When a victim gets close enough, the mantis lunges forward to grab its next meal.

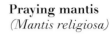

Praying mantis
(Mantis religiosa)

Grasshopper
(Acrididae)

◀ ONE GIANT LEAP

Grasshoppers escape from their enemies by leaping, as this one is doing. These insects have two pairs of wings but are not strong fliers. They can cover up to 1m (3ft) in one single bound. Before it leaps, the grasshopper gathers its strong hind legs under its body. Muscles then pull on the upper and lower legs to straighten the limbs and hurl the insect into the air.

FLOWER DISGUISE ▶

Mantids use their camouflage to hunt down their prey. This beautiful tropical 'flower' is actually a flower mantis. These amazing insects have flaps on their legs and heads that resemble the petals of flowers. Some mantids mimic green or dying leaves.

◀ SINGING

This male grasshopper is stridulating (singing) to attract a female. He produces a stream of high-pitched rasping sounds by rubbing his hind legs against his front wings. Crickets sing in a slightly different way – they rub rough patches on their wings together. These insects can detect sound through special 'ears' on their legs or abdomens.

Beetles, Bugs and People

Beetles and bugs do many useful jobs that benefit people, either directly or indirectly. They fertilize plants and consume waste matter. They also provide a valuable food source for many other animals, including reptiles and birds.

However, most people regard many beetles and bugs as pests because they can harm us or our lands and possessions. Aphids, chafers and weevils attack cropfields, orchards, vegetable plots and gardens. Woodboring beetles damage timber, furniture, carpets and clothes. Blood-sucking bugs harm humans and livestock, and some carry dangerous diseases, such as malaria. People wage war against these pests – and many other harmless beetles and bugs. Some species are in danger of dying out altogether because people are killing them, or destroying the places in which they live.

▲ CARPET-CRUNCHER
A carpet beetle larva munches on a woollen carpet. These young beetles become pests when they hatch out on carpets and clothes. The larvae have spines on their bodies that protect them from enemies. A close relative, the museum beetle, also causes havoc. It eats its way through preserved animal specimens in museums.

COLLECTING INSECTS ▶
If you are collecting insects, remember to handle them carefully so that you do not damage them. Always return insects to the place where you found them. Do not try to catch delicate insects such as dragonflies, or ones that could sting you, such as wasps.

▲ DUTCH ELM DISEASE

Elm bark beetles (*Scolytus scolytus*) are wood-borers. The fungus they carry causes Dutch elm disease, which kills elm trees. During the 1970s, a major outbreak of the disease destroyed most of the elm trees in Britain.

Manna from Heaven
The Old Testament of the Bible tells how the ancient Israelites survived in the desert by eating 'manna'. After many centuries of debate, historians now believe this strange food may have been scale insects, living on tamarisk trees.

▲ WOODWORM DAMAGE

This chair has fallen prey to woodworm. These beetles (Anobiidae family) can literally reduce wood to powder. Laid as eggs inside the timber, the young feed on the wood until they are ready to pupate. As winged adults, they quickly bore their way to freedom, leaving tell-tale exit holes in the wood.

▲ GARDENERS' FRIEND

These black bean aphids (*Aphis fabae*) are infested with tiny parasitic wasps. The female wasp lays her eggs on the aphids. When the young hatch, they eat the bugs. Gardeners consider aphids a pest and welcome the wasps in their gardens. Wasps are sometimes used in large numbers by gardeners to control pests.

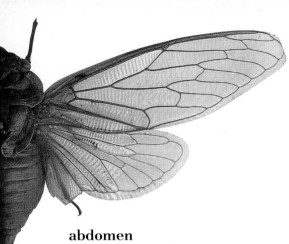

GLOSSARY

abdomen
The rear section of an insect's body, which holds the reproductive organs and part of the digestive system.

adapt
When an animal, or group of animals, changes in order to survive in new conditions.

antennae (singular: antenna)
The 'feelers' on top of an insect's head, which are used for smelling, touching and tasting.

camouflage
The coloration and patterns on an animal's body that blend in with its surroundings, allowing it to hide from its enemies or creep up on its prey.

carnivore
An animal that feeds on the flesh of other animals.

carrion
Remains of a dead animal.

cocoon
Another term for a pupa.

compound eyes
The large eyes found on many insects, which are made up of many lenses.

cuticle
The tough substance that forms the outer skin of an insect.

diet
The range of food an animal eats.

elytra (singular: elytron)
The hardened wing cases of a beetle that have evolved from the insect's front wings. When the beetle is on the ground, the elytra fold over and protect its delicate back wings.

evolve
When a species of animal changes gradually over many generations to become better suited to the conditions in which it lives.

exoskeleton
The tough shell of an insect's body, which acts like a skeleton and protects the soft parts inside.

extinct
When a whole species of animal has died out completely.

family
A scientific classification grouping together related animals or plants. Families are sub-divided into genera.

fertile
An animal that is able to produce young after mating.

fossil
The preserved remains of a plant or animal, usually found in rocks.

genus (plural: genera)
A scientific classification grouping together related animals or plants. Genera are sub-divided into species.

gill
Part of an animal's body used for breathing underwater. Insects' gills are often feathery.

habitat
A type of place where certain animals and plants live, such as a tropical rainforest or a desert.

halteres
The balancing organs of flies. Halteres are the remnants of the hind wings and look like tiny drumsticks.

invertebrate
An animal without an internal skeleton. Insects, which have an exoskeleton, are invertebrates.

larva (plural: larvae)
The young of insects that undergo complete metamorphosis, such as beetles, butterflies and true flies. Larvae can be grubs, caterpillars or maggots.

lens
Part of an animal's eye, which helps it to see.

life cycle
Series of stages in the life of an insect as it grows up and becomes an adult.

mammal
A warm-blooded animal with a bony skeleton. Mammals feed their young on milk.

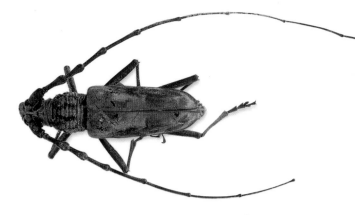

mating
When a male and female animal come together to produce young.

metamorphosis
The transformation of a young insect into an adult. Beetles have four stages in their life cycle: egg, larva, pupa and adult. This is called complete metamorphosis. Bugs have only three stages in their life cycle: egg, nymph and adult. They undergo incomplete metamorphosis.

minibeast
Insects and similar small animals such as spiders, wood lice, scorpions and centipedes.

moult
When a young, growing insect sheds its skin and grows a new, larger one.

nocturnal
Describes an animal that rests by day and is active during the hours of darkness.

nymph
The young of insects which undergo incomplete metamorphosis, such as bugs, grasshoppers and dragonflies.

order
A scientific category. Beetles and bugs are two orders of insects. Orders are sub-divided into families.

parasite
An animal that lives on, or in, another animal and obtains its food from it without killing it.

parthenogenesis
The process by which some female insects can reproduce without mating.

predator
An animal that hunts and eats other animals for food.

pupa (plural: pupae)
The protective case that forms the third stage in a beetle's life cycle, before it becomes an adult.

rostrum
The long snout of a weevil.

scavenger
An animal that feeds on rubbish and the remains of dead animals.

simple eyes
Small, bead-like eyes found on an insect's head that can detect light and dark.

social
Describes an animal that lives with others of its species in a cooperative group.

species
A particular type of animal or plant. The Goliath beetle is a species of beetle.

spiracles
The holes in the sides of an insect's body through which air passes into breathing tubes.

stridulate
When an insect produces sound by rubbing parts of the body together.

territory
An area that an animal uses for feeding or breeding. Animals will defend their territory against others of its species.

thorax
The middle section of an insect's body. The insect's wings and legs are attached to the thorax.

veins
The thin, hollow tubes which support an insect's wings.

warning colours
Distinctive coloration, often combinations of red, yellow and black, which are common to many foul-tasting or poisonous animals, and which warn predators away.

INDEX

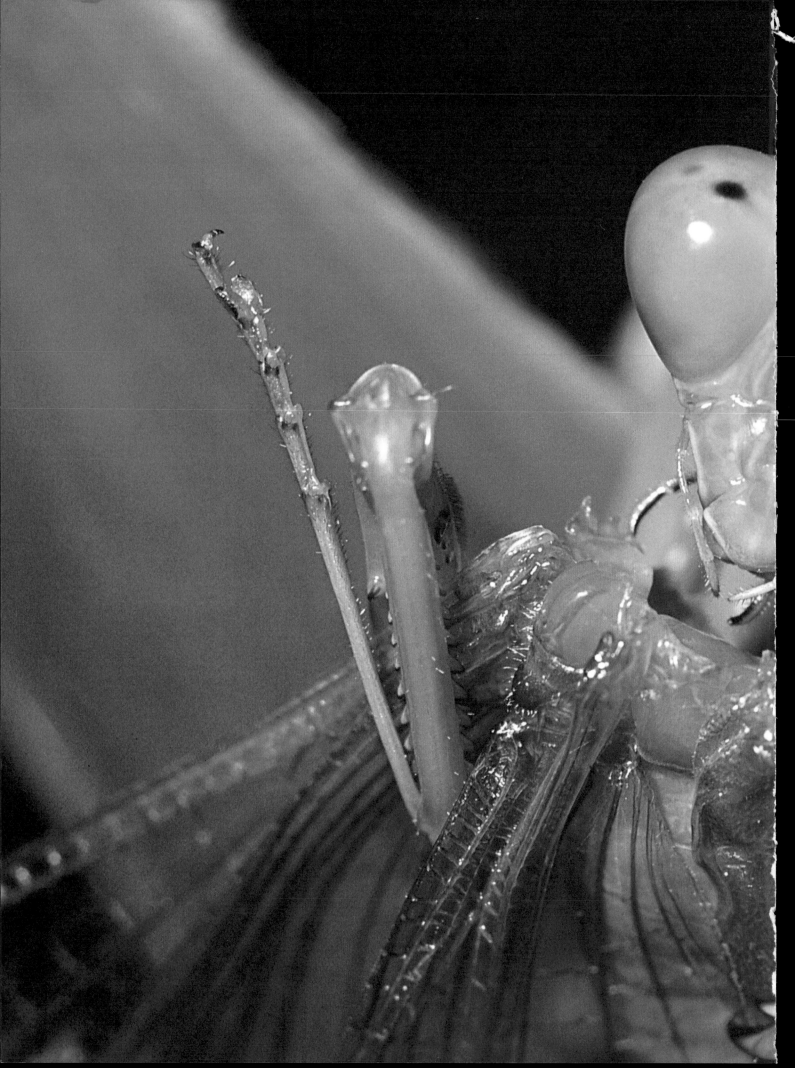